Books by Bob Gill

F/F/G 1962
  written with Alan Fletcher and Colin Forbes
Graphic Design: Visual Comparisons 1963
  written with Alan Fletcher and Colin Forbes
Illustration: Aspects and Directions 1964
  written with John Lewis
Bob Gill's Portfolio 1968
*Forget all the rules you ever learned about graphic design
  including the ones in this book* 1982
Graphic Design Made Difficult 1992
Unspecial Effects for Graphic Designers 2001
Graphic Design as a Second Language 2003
Illustration 2004
LogoMania 2006
Words into Pictures 2009

For Children

The Millionaires 1959
  written with Alastair Reid
A Balloon for a Blunderbuss 1961
  written with Alastair Reid
  reprinted 2008
What Colour is Your World? 1962
  reprinted 2008
A to Z 1962
  to be reprinted 2009
The Present 1963
  written with Alan Fletcher and Colin Forbes
*The Green Eyed Mouse and the
  Blue Eyed Mouse* 1965
  to be reprinted 2009
Parade 1968
  written with Keith Botsworth
I Keep Changing 1971
  written with Alastair Reid
  reprinted 2008
The Ups and the Downs 1972
  to be reprinted 2009

Bob Gill

**Words
into
Pictures**

images
Publishing

Published in Australia in 2009 by
The Images Publishing Group Pty Ltd
ABN 89 059 734 431
6 Bastow Place, Mulgrave, Victoria 3170, Australia
Tel: +61 3 9561 5544 Fax: +61 3 9561 4860
books@imagespublishing.com
www.imagespublishing.com

Copyright © The Images Publishing Group Pty Ltd 2009
The Images Publishing Group Reference Number: 836

National Library of Australia Cataloguing-in-Publication entry:
Author: Gill, Bob, 1931–
Title: Words into pictures / Bob Gill.
ISBN: 9781864703269 (hbk.)
Subjects: Gill, Bob, 1931– —Pictorial works.
   Graphic arts—Pictorial works.
   Graphic design (Typography)—Pictorial works.
   Graphic artists.
   Visual communication.
   Words in art.
Dewey Number: 760.092

Design: Bob Gill
Digital Artwork: Jack Gill
Pre-press: Ashish Shal

Coordinating editor: Beth Browne

Digital production by The Graphic Image Studio, Pty Ltd, Australia
www.tgis.com.au

Printed on 140 gsm GoldEast Matt Art
by Everbest Printing Co. Ltd., in Hong Kong/China

Scribes and poets have been creating works with both literary and visual interest since ancient times.

What fascinates me about this genre is that it has the potential to be the simplest and most original way of communicating.

Why show the name of something and then have to make it *look* interesting by adding an image when the two functions can be combined?

Less is more.

More can also be more. But, for the purposes of this book, turning words into pictures, less is certainly more.

DSB

The initials DSB form the logo of the Danish State Railway.

Obviously, the Railway wants to project an image of modernity. The modern typeface does that. But is that enough for a logo … just an appropriate typeface?

The Mazda of Japan logo is a bit more ambitious.

Rather than simply choosing existing letter forms, in this case, the designer created unique ones.

Better.

But the logo could still do more. It could say something about its products or its mission.

If we limit ourselves to choosing appropriate typefaces, or even modifying existing ones so that they reflect the hottest typographic fashions, we deprive ourselves of the chance to create unique images and to have genuinely new experiences with every new job.

Although I don't presume to speak for the other 52 designers that keep me company in this collection, I suspect, as we change words into pictures, we use a similar process:

We don't think about design, until we have something to say (an idea) about the subject of the job.

After we have an idea, we let the idea *suggest* how the solution should look.

We don't have to limit ourselves to what the "culture" tells us is fashionable.

We believe that what is *good design* is what communicates best, even though it doesn't conform to what we are told is *good design*.

Early examples of this genre are on the next six pages.

And then, the modern collection begins on page 12.

I also included a few *non-idea* examples that I admire, on pages 120 to 124.

The credits run from pages 126 to 128.

Enjoy.

A pictorial alphabet from France
dated 1596.

A   B   C   D

I   K   L   M

R   S   T   V

E   F   G   H

N   O   P   Q

W   X   Y   Z

Poets and writers in Victorian England were very interested in *shaped* works.

Lewis Carroll's *The Mouse's Tale* from *Alice's Adventures in Wonderland* from 1865 is an example.

We lived beneath the mat,
        Warm and snug and fat,
                But one woe, and that
                        Was the Cat!

                        ———

                                To our joys
                                a clog, In
                        our eyes a
                fog, On our
        hearts a log,
    Was the Dog!

                        ———

        When the
    Cat's away,
        Then
    The mice
        will
            play,
                But alas!
                    one day, (So they say)

                        ———

                Came the Dog and
                Cat, hunting
                    for a
                    Rat,
                Crushed
                the mice
            all flat,
        Each
    one
        as
            he
            sat,
                Underneath
                    the mat, Warm
                        and snug and fat,
                            Think of
                            that!

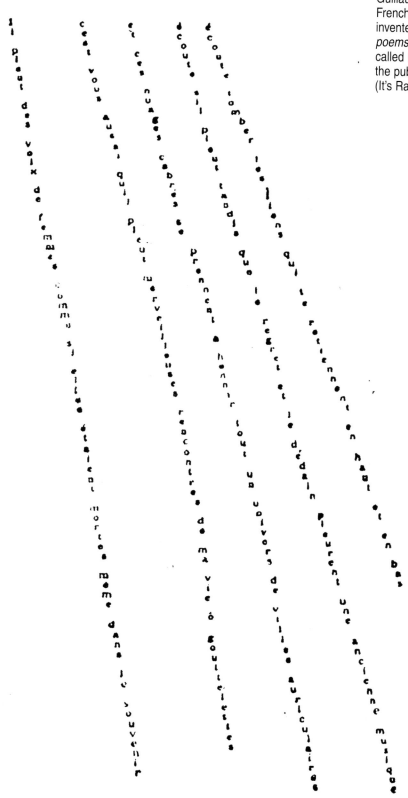

Guillaume Apollinaire, the French Dadaist, claimed he invented modernist *shaped poems* in 1918, which he called *Calligrammes* with the publication of *Il Pleut* (It's Raining).

Closer to our own time, is the
ubiquitous ice machine lettering.

And the nervous lettering in every horror comic book, which I used in an ad for an inexpensive canoe trip.

And finally, this short history
ends with some typical WWII
patriotic lettering.

The earliest in this collection is from the 1950s, and the most recent is from a few weeks ago.

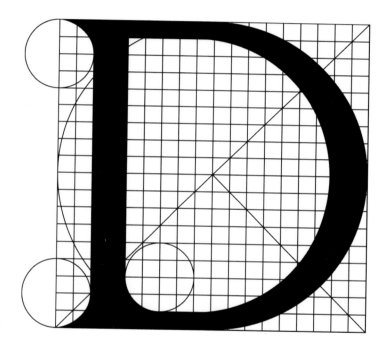

Drawing:
for no particular job, just for fun.

Logo:
Ocean Oil Company.

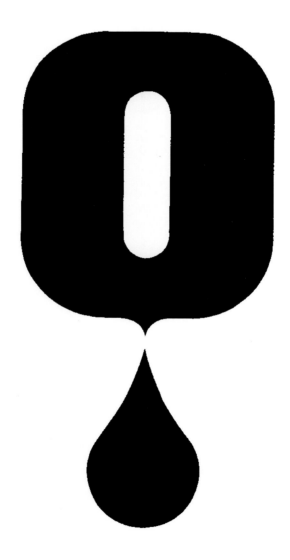

TONNAGE

When is a heavy weight of advertising dollars bound to succeed? And when is "Tonnage" bound to fail? Is the smartest advertiser the one with the biggest budget? If you look at the history of advertising, you will observe the following facts: There are advertisers who slackened, or weakened their efforts (sometimes at critical times) and the results can be seen in the forgotten trademarks of the past. On the other hand, there are advertisers who mounted massive advertising campaigns—costing many millions of dollars—who have failed to increase their sales. The question of the advertising appropriation should always be preceded by these questions: Do I have an idea which will sell my product? Has my agency been thorough enough to arrive at a sound selling strategy, and ingenious enough to express it in an arresting and interesting way? If the answers to these questions are "yes," advertising tonnage can be regarded as an investment, instead of an expense. Everything depends on the idea. Ideas sell products because—people buy ideas.

YOUNG & RUBICAM · ADVERTISING

Logo:
Freud Year, 2006.
Sigmund Freud Museum,
Vienna.

Logo:
American Physicians' Fellowship,
consisting of American and
Israeli doctors.

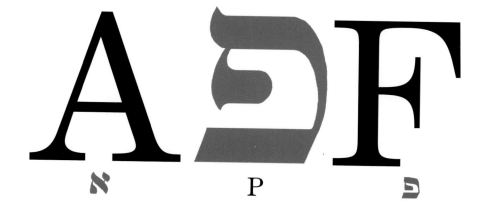

Logo:
Irwin Studios.

Logo:
series of informal luncheons
for the United Nations
Association.

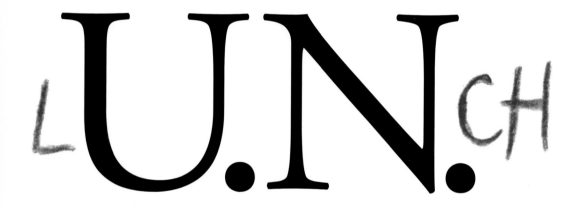

Logo:
Provo Allergy & Asthma Clinic

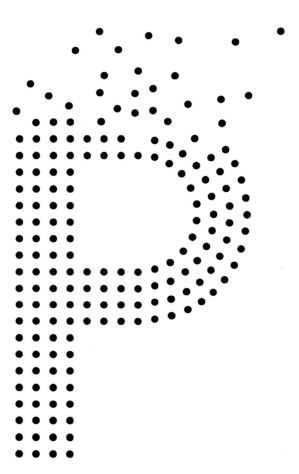

Logo:
television film series with
contemporary themes related to
the Ten Commandments.

Logo:
series of radio programs about
immigration in the beginning of
the last century.

The photographs are from the
museum on Ellis Island.

Logo:
Ellen Designs.

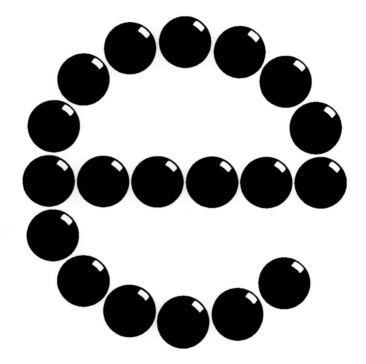

Logo:
series of programs for
public television.
.

Logo:
Fine Line Features.

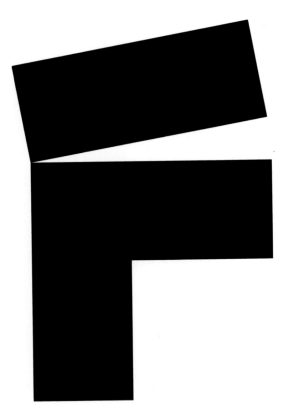

Logo:
The Friederichs Heyking Steel
Company.

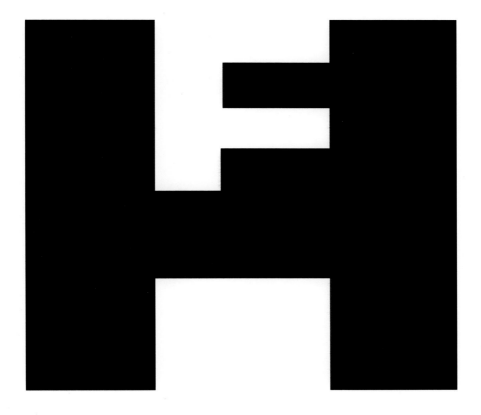

Book cover: detail.
An analysis of the British press.

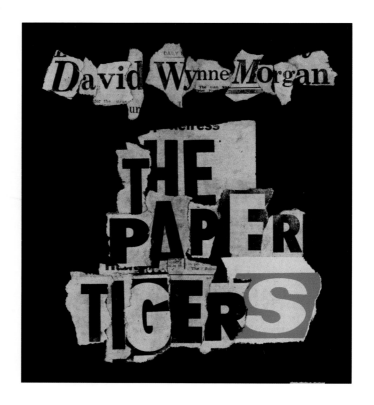

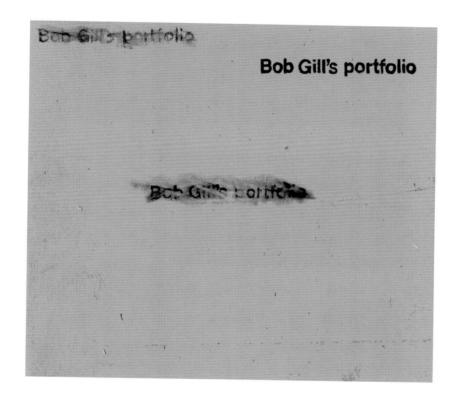

Logo:
Fidelity Group of Funds,
represented by a bar graph.

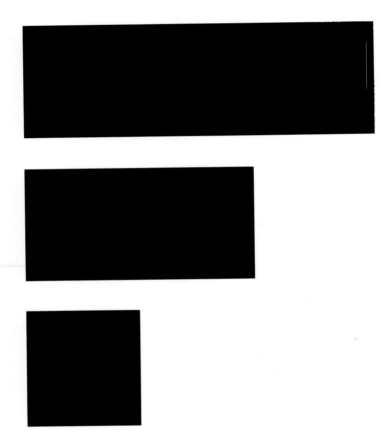

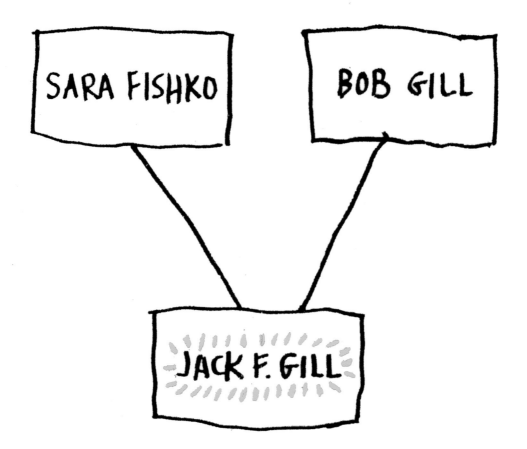

Real estate ad headline.
The ad is about the glamour of
Broadway properties.

Logo:
Television Associates, Ltd.

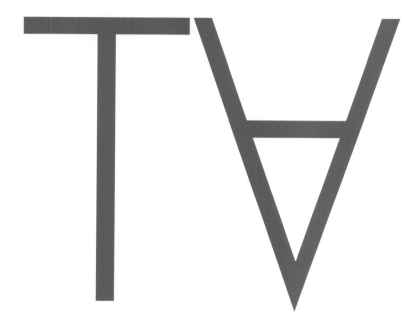

Logo:
national chain of opticians.

Logo:
John Page, sound recordist.

jŏn pāj sownd

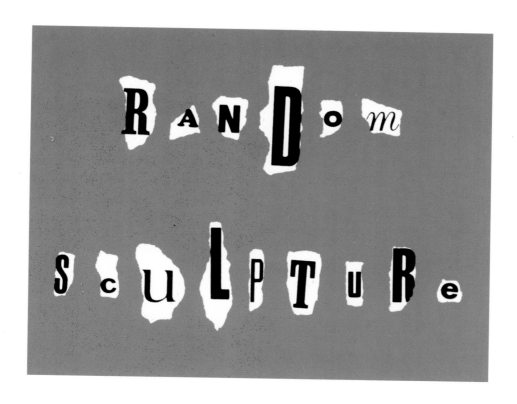

Logo:
Brian Harvey, architect.

20% off

Martin

RentaCa

If you are unhappy with your present silkscreen and display services

Identity:
Architecture Week for
The Arts Council of Great Britain.

ARCHITECTURE

Logo:
Robert Rabinowitz, consultant.
(Maven means *expert* in Yiddish.)

Management!
and!
Publicity!
Limited!

Exhibition announcement detail.

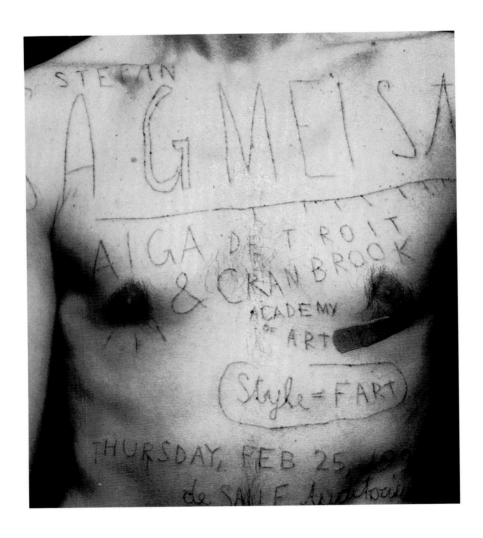

Trade ad detail:
film about gangs in Los Angeles.

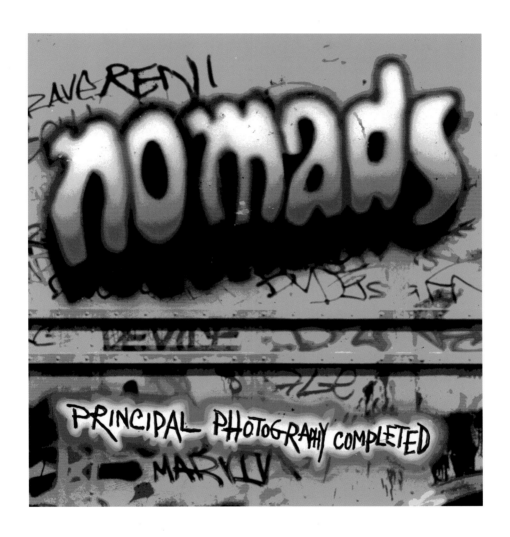

Ad detail:
Bergdorf Goodman.

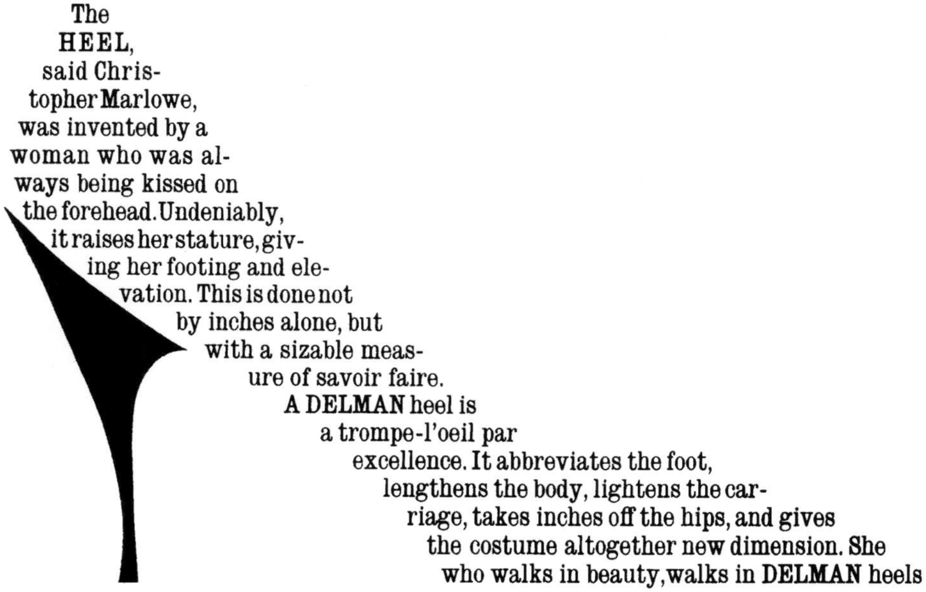

The
HEEL,
said Chris-
topher Marlowe,
was invented by a
woman who was al-
ways being kissed on
the forehead. Undeniably,
it raises her stature, giv-
ing her footing and ele-
vation. This is done not
by inches alone, but
with a sizable meas-
ure of savoir faire.
A DELMAN heel is
a trompe-l'oeil par
excellence. It abbreviates the foot,
lengthens the body, lightens the car-
riage, takes inches off the hips, and gives
the costume altogether new dimension. She
who walks in beauty, walks in **DELMAN** heels

58

MARTY
PATTON
HAMLET
BEN-HUR
ROCKY
WINGS
GIGI
ANNIE HALL
GOING MY WAY
AN AMERICAN IN PARIS
A MAN FOR ALL SEASONS
IN THE HEAT OF THE NIGHT
HOW GREEN WAS MY VALLEY
IT HAPPENED ONE NIGHT
MUTINY ON THE BOUNTY
TERMS OF ENDEARMENT
FROM HERE TO ETERNITY
GENTLEMAN'S AGREEMENT
THE LOST WEEKEND
ALL THE KING'S MEN
CHARIOTS OF FIRE
ALL ABOUT EVE
MY FAIR LADY
GRAND HOTEL
THE GODFATHER
SCHINDLER'S LIST
ORDINARY PEOPLE
THE LAST EMPEROR
WEST SIDE STORY
OUT OF AFRICA
FORREST GUMP
CASABLANCA
TOM JONES
CIMARRON
MRS. MINIVER
UNFORGIVEN
CAVALCADE
RAIN MAN
THE STING
OLIVER!
AMADEUS
PLATOON
REBECCA
GANDHI
BRAVEHEART
THE LIFE OF EMILE ZOLA
MIDNIGHT COWBOY
ON THE WATERFRONT
THE SILENCE OF THE LAMBS
AROUND THE WORLD IN 80 DAYS
THE BEST YEARS OF OUR LIVES
LAWRENCE OF ARABIA
THE BRIDGE ON THE RIVER KWAI
YOU CAN'T TAKE IT WITH YOU
THE FRENCH CONNECTION
ALL QUIET ON THE WESTERN FRONT
THE GREATEST SHOW ON EARTH
ONE FLEW OVER THE CUCKOO'S NEST
DRIVING MISS DAISY * THE SOUND OF MUSIC
THE GODFATHER PART II * KRAMER VS. KRAMER
GONE WITH THE WIND * THE APARTMENT
DANCES WITH WOLVES * THE DEER HUNTER
THE GREAT ZIEGFELD * THE BROADWAY MELODY
69TH ANNUAL ACADEMY AWARDS®

House number for personal
stationery bought in a local
hardware store.

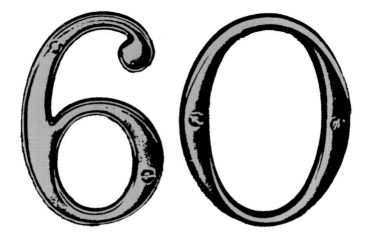

House number for personal
stationery of an American
expatriate living in Paris, also
from a local hardware store.

Logo:
Purser & Company. The dovetail
joint represents their cabinet
making business.

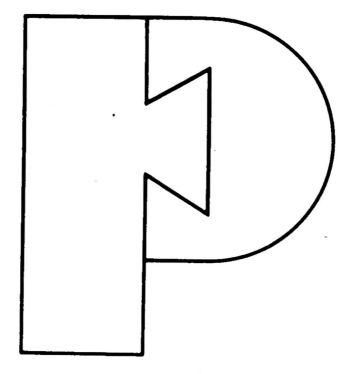

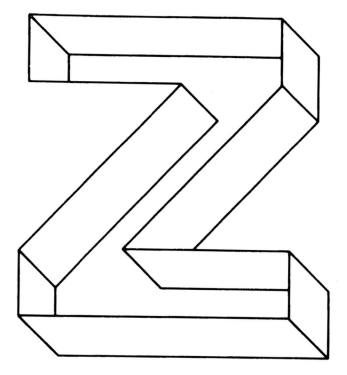

Drawing:
no particular job, just for fun.

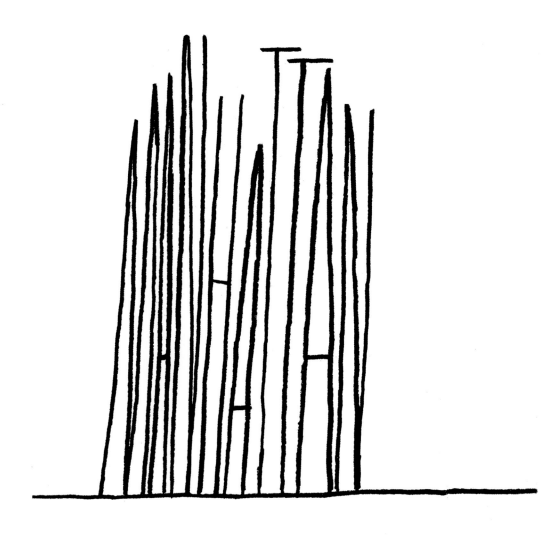

A&Fe

Logo:
a play based on Lewis Carroll's
children's story.

The logo is always shown as a
mirror image; theatre marquee,
program cover, posters, ads, etc.

ecilA

Logo:
Elektra Entertainment.

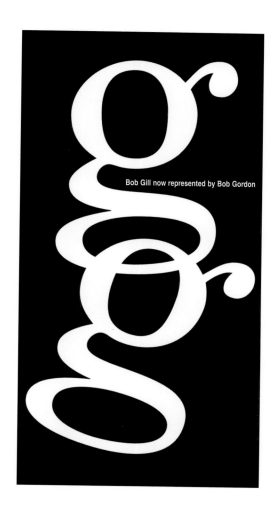

Bob Gill now represented by Bob Gordon

Logo:
Reuters International News Agency.

Logo:
event planning company.

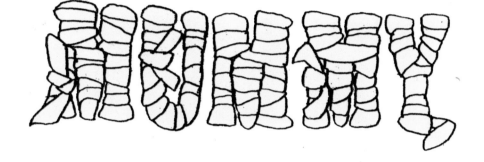

Logo:
Ealing Electro Optics.

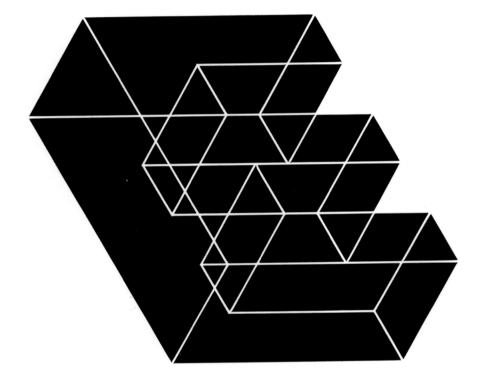

Typographica magazine feature:
"Type talks."

ha

lf

addding
subtrcting
multimultiplying
div id ing

aboutface

leaning

st len

o
ver

dead

tophalf

temperature

per.od
com,ma
c:l:n

enc

ero

s   t op!

1ne

2wo

3hree

sexxx

4our

5ive   f_oor   clim

Illustration:
9/11, *The New York Times.*

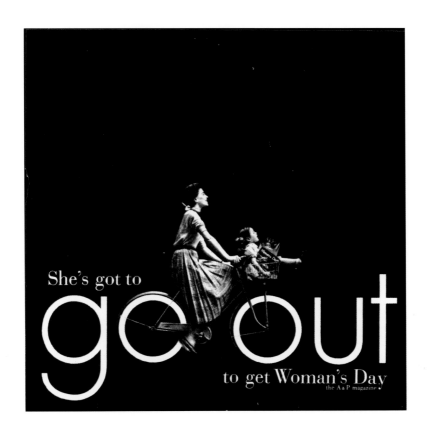

Logo:
Stravinsky Festival Trust.

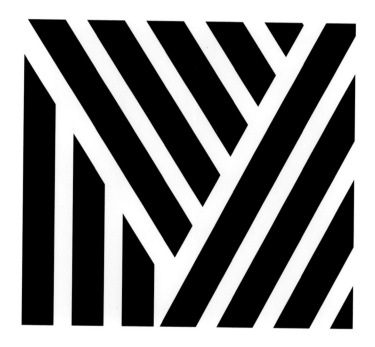

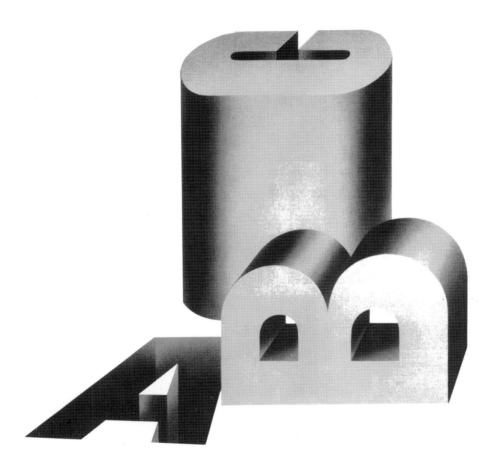

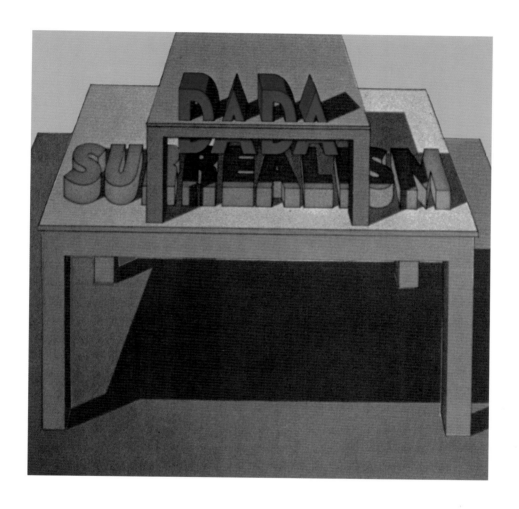

Logo:
Holtzapfel Furniture Company.

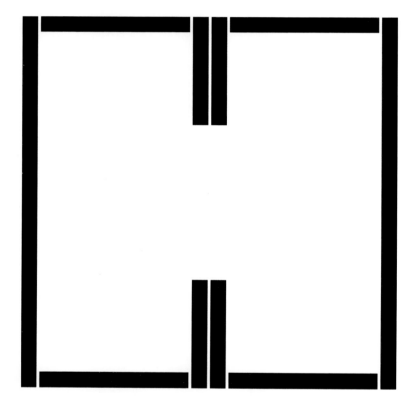

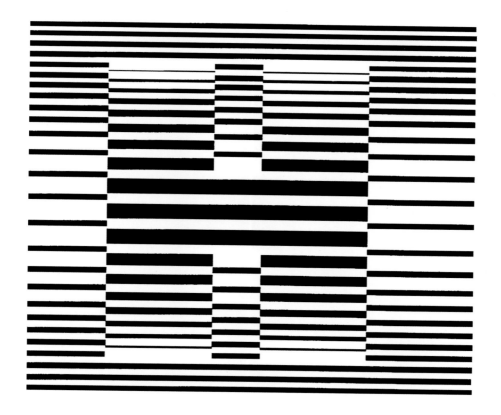

Logo:
comedy about a character who
is injured in an accident.

Anti-apartheid newspaper
masthead.

~~apartheid~~ news

Logo:
Fund for Survival.

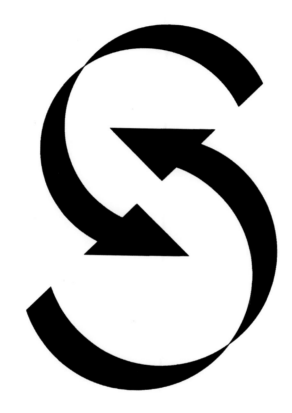

Logo:
London International Festival
of Theatre.

Logo:
The Datum Group. Inc.

Book cover:
Simon & Schuster.

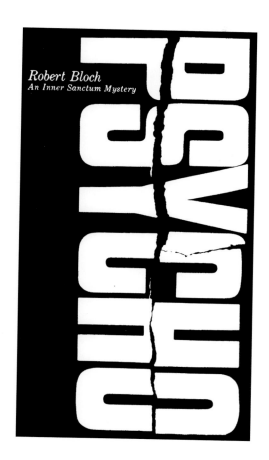

Magazine illustration:
The Nation:
"European Ecomomic Gloom."

Logo:
Applied Minds, Inc.,
a *think tank*.

Logo:
Testosterone Deficiency
Disease Foundation.

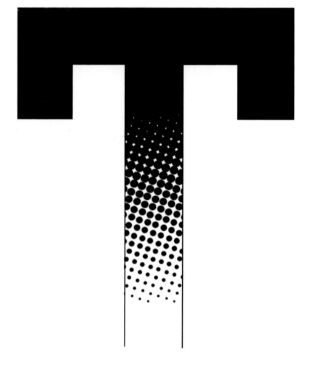

Logo:
TV commercial
editing company.

Album cover detail:
RSO Records.

Logo:
Shiseido of Japan,
inspired by a game.

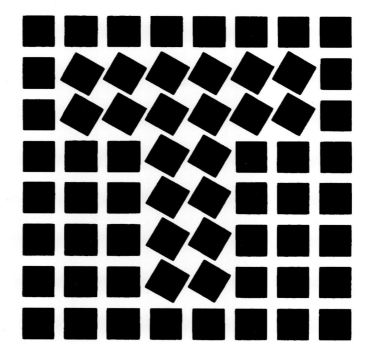

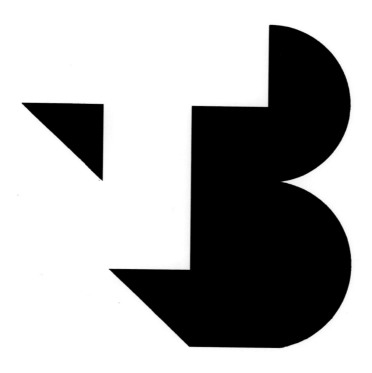

Museum poster detail.

Book cover detail:
E.P. Dutton Publishers.

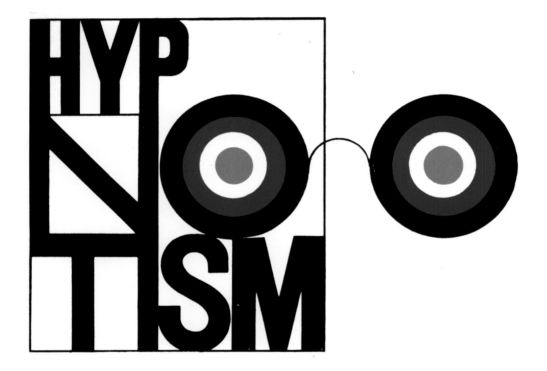

Logo:
Hair family.

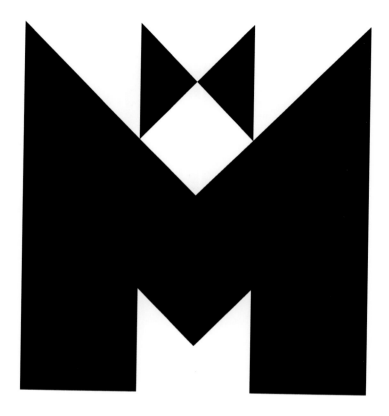

Double page spread:
diary with contradictory images:
The New York Times.

Pharmaceutical ad detail:
Dimitone.

allergic

SWELLING

Logo:
chain of cafés.

ZUM
ZUM

Ad detail:
CBS Radio.

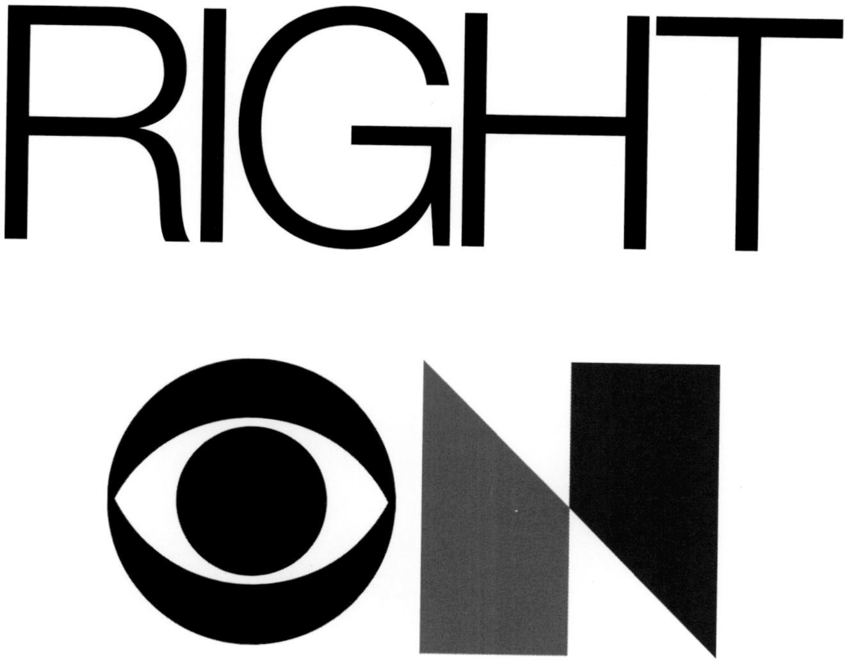

On the other hand...

What a boring typographic world
we would inhabit, if every job
consisted of an *interesting idea.*

While I spend almost all of my
time (possibly obsessed), with
conceptual graphics, I get
pleasure, and inspiration from
work concerned only with how it
looks. (Pages 120 through 124.)

One of the few times that I tried
solving a problem with a
non-idea was for a publisher's
logo. (See page 123.)

They hated it.

That's the last time I ever tried
presenting a non-idea idea.

Poster:
Museo Cantonale d'Arte,
Lugano, Italy.

Catalog cover:
The Art Institute of Chicago.

20th century *A*rt.

*A*rensberg collection.

Credits